ISBN-13:
978-0692084960 (Woodrow Claybon III)

ISBN-10:
0692084967

Native to Nowhere

Written By: Woodrow Claybon III

For myself.

Contents

1. Introduction

My name is Woodrow Claybon III. My vintage first name punctuates my old-fashioned upbringing on the south side of Chicago. I have two nurturing parents that sacrificed so that I could elevate myself in capitalist America; the America that prides itself in its freedom and justice "for all." I am another black male that wants to confront some of the persecutions that I have experienced merely because of who I am. Another black male who has spent a significant amount of time in introspection and has produced art from his pain, his lessons, and his victories. I want to share my stories because I want my readers to find familiarity in my words. I realize that I am one of many who struggle in understanding their identity and position in society.

Much of my poetry was written as I sorted through my own struggles with identity. Who was I? Who was I supposed to be? Who has the right to dictate this image? Each poem was an answer to a question that had been burning in my brain. A declaration of understanding. My writing helped me process and heal from trauma, it helped me materialize my emotions, and track my progression. Upon graduating from undergrad a few months ago, I knew that I no longer owed the world an explanation. I had already beat the odds, but I knew that I couldn't revel in complacency. Instead, I was responsible for reaching out my hand to help those who fight similar battles. Those who are also trying to answer their own burning questions to themselves.

In the early stages, I asked myself why I was writing. Above all else, I want my book to trigger conversation. Conversation in the home, in the church, even in the workplace. I want people to begin to address some of the ongoing issues that we are having in the African American community, as well as the issues that persist in imperialist, white-supremacist, capitalist America. As much as I would love for these to be buzzwords that could never hurt me, they are instead the sticks and stones that have broken the bones of many. I want these issues to be interpreted and digested within our communities, and I want to promote collective healing. There are anti-minority systems in place that will take years to dismantle, but that process will never start without a conversation. The conversation starts with you. Your experiences and your contributions are valid. We, collectively, are a mosaic of colors screaming at the top of our lungs to be heard in monochromatic America. The America that appropriates and embraces us only when it is convenient to do so.

In all honesty, there are times when I want to accept and conform to the expectations that are redundantly present in my daily life. Being reduced to a threat. An unintelligible beast that preys on women and thrives in criminal activity. A misunderstood catastrophe that would be better off locked away. A man that remains a product of poverty and lack of resources. A man who doesn't aspire, but instead only concerns himself with the issues of the day at hand. Yes. Why not succumb to what America expects me to be? Why not shut my negro mouth and cling to the Eurocentric Christian culture that was imposed on us? I refuse to keep quiet because there were many that came before me that died so that I could have a choice. I have a choice in who I want to be and what I want to say.

My job is to share my story. To add to the literature that has been so diligently produced by those before me. At twenty-two years old, my perspective is still broadening, but my input is valid. I have witnessed my own transitions first hand. I am rich clay that is continuously molding in the hands of many. The hands of my lovers. The hands of my persecutors. The hands of my support system. Most importantly, the hands of God Himself. The molding never ends, meaning that any part of the process can be appreciated.

Like many, I made the mistake of trying to establish my identity based on external expectations. I wasted copious amounts of energy trying to deny my true self. Trying to disown my purpose. Many people go their whole lives being a slave to identity theft. It is no secret that the livelihood of minorities, women, and the LGBTQ+ are not prioritized around the world. We are constantly fighting for (adequate) representation. It is easy to cower into conformity considering the amount of external pressure that exists. It's easier to stay quiet.

There are so many things that divide us as human beings – race, religion, sex, gender, sexuality, age, political view, economic status, disability…and the list goes on. All of these elements grow the gaps between us, creating unnecessary barriers. However, I believe that our experiences as human beings bridge many of those gaps. As we realize that people have comparable experiences, we begin to dismantle some of the barriers that stifle the progression of the human race.

I am committed to sharing my work because I want people to reconsider their perceptions. Hopefully after reading this book, you'll carry more love for yourself, and more appreciation for the people you have around you.

-   Woodrow/ Red/ tbd

Are you building bridges, or are you building barriers?

2. Yesterday's Gold

I can remember one of my history teachers in high school becoming frustrated with the lack of interest in the classroom. She commanded the attention of the class and uttered, "You guys need history! We need to understand the past in order to understand the present!" At that point in my life, I could only chuckle at her conviction. But she was so right. The older I get, the more I prioritize reflection. As I review certain events from my past, I think about the lessons that I have attained from them. Understanding how my past has impacted my character and my perception gives me clarity about the present.

I am beyond guilty of thinking about my past in my daydreaming. I've zoned out in interviews, prayer, while driving, 3 minutes ago…whatever, judge me later. It doesn't help that I have the attention span of a rat. I'm always catapulting back into moments in the past where I felt safe or at home. Nostalgia is one of the best drugs. Plus, the present is overrated, a gamble if nothing else. It's easier for me to bury myself into my memories and face the present with a 10 foot pole. But if I'm not careful, I'll get trapped in a binge of reflection, and begin to apply trivial occurrences of the past to my current life. I'll give you an example of my path of thoughts:

me to myself
"Wow why can't I be a kindergartener again? Life was easy. Oh shit. I had a best friend in kindergarten named Andrew (named changed for privacy purposes). One day, Andrew peed on himself in class. Some of our classmates laughed at him. I laughed too. A real friend would have told the other classmates to shut up. Does that make me a fake friend? Am I even capable of being a real friend?"
And then begins an intense evaluation of the authenticity of my current friendships. I know guys, I wish I could say that I was exaggerating.
But on a more serious note, it is important to indulge in introspection from time to time. Without memory, we would not be able to consolidate knowledge about survival. Our memories serve as reservoirs for our learning and development.

Old Flame

I've acquainted with
All of today's older sisters
And I have found a few
That I will never forget

Past

My sweet yesterday
Somehow, I had grown eyes for you in the back of my
head
Mother of memories, you have swaddled your child in
nostalgia

Thoughts of you cloud the stratosphere of my mind
You have been kind to me in retrospect
But as I introspect the traces of you terrorize my travels

I am a nomad, moving through your immobility
I don't want to get stuck in you
My carnality tells me that I am hungry for comfort
You, sweet yesterday, are my low hanging fruit

Growing on trees in the West Indies
I am left searching for you on islands of isolation
The way I hang onto you quietly implies that somehow I
can even
Romanticize the parts of you that I once despised

Time has stolen me from you over and over again, my
lover
Imagine only being held by you, when I am being held
back

Sweet yesterday
You are the pigments in my skin
My complexion has become contraception
and freedom can no longer be born

You are the distant constellation of dim stars
I know you'll never come back to me

Excuse me past, but I need to get past you

Zennie

During the first half of my childhood, I lived with my mother in a bungalow in Beverly, a treasured neighborhood on the south side of Chicago. Our home was nestled into a quiet cul-de-sac that occasionally enticed drivers looking for shortcuts. Sometimes I would look out of my front window and see cars zip down the street, only to return in the opposite direction moments later.

At some point after age 7 or 8, my grandmother Zennie moved in with us. My mother often worked until 5 and would get home around 6, but I would get home from school around 3. My grandmother would look after me until my mother returned home from her job. She had a liberal approach to looking after me, and I would arrive home from school with excitement (knowing that I could do things that my mother wouldn't normally let me indulge in). As long as my homework was completed (her interpretation of complete was me telling her it was complete), I could raid the kitchen for snacks and watch television. We would often play checkers, and she would sometimes move her pieces with intent to let me win. When I would jump one of her pieces that she had "forgotten" to protect, she would gasp in disbelief and say "WHAT? Boy, you're getting good at this." She taught me that sometimes you need to let people win, so that they know it's possible for them.

We had two shows that we would watch religiously, as if the solidarity of our relationship depended on it. *Ripley's Believe it or Not* and *King of Queens*. I would reach into our kitchen cabinet and dig around for microwave popcorn. Looking back, I wish that I had eaten less of this poisonous snack. I can remember seeing multiple news reports that declared that microwave popcorn was linked to cancer. It wasn't until my freshman year of college that I abandoned this snack; I had decided that anything that could taste that good from the microwave couldn't possibly be good for you.

Zennie was an avid conversationalist, but her wisdom would even radiate from her silence. She would peruse her tattered Bible as if she had read it a million times. She was one of the few people I've met that have actually learned from this book. *She applied it to herself more than she applied it to others.*

My last fond memory of her was washing greens together on a warm summer day. This monotonous task was the highlight of my day because I was alongside one of the greatest women I had ever met. I thought about all the greens she must've washed in her lifetime. Even so, she approached the sink with a loyal grin. We chattered about current events that she didn't understand, and she would interlude with stories about her own life. I clung to these stories because I wanted them to be mine as well. I can remember her washing the leaves of the greens so efficiently, and I wondered how she could be that meticulous at her age.

Although she moved at more relaxed pace, you could still see the intent in her eyes. As we finished washing the last of the greens, there was a silence that fell upon us. After a few moments, she began to hum softly to herself. I will never forget this sound. The greens sloshing in the water. The birds chirping outside our back door. Her song. I could never pick up what the song was, but it was beautiful. In that moment, nothing else mattered except the energy she was creating.

During the time that we spent together, I challenged myself to mimic her kindness. I have always been mild-tempered and laid back, but I wanted to exude the same compassionate energy that she had. Loving a person beyond their labels. Asking about their day and listening to what happened in it. Encouraging and pushing. She was iron sharpening iron. This is the energy that I have insatiable thirst for. The energy that I wanted to project from my body everywhere I go. If the world had more of this energy, more people would be safe and content.

As I grew older, her health began to deteriorate. She began to make frequent trips to the hospital and eventually she was placed into a nursing home. Many people hesitate to place their loved ones into nursing homes because they can be very depressing and isolating. However, my family and I would visit Zennie often (in retrospect, it seems like she had a visitor almost daily). Even within the nursing home, her spirit was warm and inviting. She was able to come home for Christmas of 2007, and I can remember a large number of family members being present. After that, her conditions worsened, and we began to anticipate what we weren't nearly ready for. The summer rolled around and she passed on July 29th, 2008. That was the first time I had lost someone close to me, and I can remember being upset for a while after the funeral. My mom and the rest of the family seemed to have peace about it, but I couldn't digest losing one of my close friends.

Of course, time heals all wounds. Whenever I think of her now, I imagine that she's my guardian angel (as if she'd have nothing better to do in heaven). Sometimes I still hear her humming, or the greens sloshing in the sink. I learned a lot about the importance of interaction from her. She was a woman of broad perspective. She inspired me to seek understanding. Now in my early adulthood, I find myself reaching beyond mainstream competency. I strive to understand the people who are different than me, because I know it'll bring me closer to them. If I am understanding someone, I am loving them. I'm so glad that my grandmother took the time to understand me.

The Porch

During the second half of my childhood, my mom decided to move in with my father at his home in Roseland. The area was a lot different than the neighborhood I was accustomed to. Sometimes in the summer I would sit on my front porch; never for too long. I would watch my new neighborhood remind me, effortlessly, of how much I didn't fit. I had only flirted with some of the adversity that the people in my neighborhood experienced daily. Upon sitting on the porch, I tried to focus my attention on the sky, something everyone has had access to. Many people in my neighborhood had been robbed of their access to everything else; they couldn't understand life outside of their own fatigue. I watched people walk by, wearing their fatigue complacently. These were still MY people.

I can remember seeing boys my age yell poetic misogyny at young girls. Sometimes these women would coo to themselves or among their friends. Other times they would scurry as if they were being chased. I never knew what to expect from another male in my neighborhood. Part of me was always expecting a robbery, or verbal banter. I resented the fact that I was beginning to view them the same way that America does. As threats. But in this neighborhood, it was safer to assume the worst in everyone. Lack of resources breeds an abundance of crime. My father would say, "People are guilty until proven innocent." I learned how to read intent in the eyes of other people. With one glare, I would know if they had eaten that day, if they were hunting, or if they were just passing by. I sat on the porch and practiced this discernment. These are still MY people.

The house right across from mine bustled with frequent visitors. Most of them were faces I'd only see once or twice. The woman and her adult son that lived there were selling medicine to the neighborhood. Some of it was green. Some of it. These customers were looking for medicine that would remedy their fatigue. So was I. I would watch people leaving the house with laughter vibrating from their smiles, as if they had found gold. There were times where I wanted to dart across the street and become a customer too. I could never muster the bravery; I knew my parents could appear at the door any moment.

The son had disappeared for quite some time. He was imprisoned for selling medicine to the fatigued people. I realized that he, like many other men in my neighborhood, were perpetuating addiction. But even so, maybe if his skin was pale and white, he would have been slapped on the wrist and returned to his home in a timely fashion. These are still MY people.

Sometimes a man would stop by my house, and ask for my father. He would always be in a hurry to make enough money for his medicine. He was one of the most energetic, fatigued men I had ever seen. I would retrieve my father, and the man would ask to do work around our house for pay. Cutting the grass, trimming our bushes, or maybe washing our cars. I admired the diversity of his skillset. My father knew that the man would use the money for his medicine, but he didn't seem to care. I, who had no interest in taking on these tasks around the house myself, also didn't care. He didn't have a phone, or a car, or a watch. I pondered if he cared about the time or his location. Maybe he only cared about his medicine. The man made me want to chase dreams outside of the noisy streets of my neighborhood. I told myself that when I did, I would come back for him, and others. These are still MY people.

I began to see these faces as my family, cousins that might have lost their way. Not everyone was comfortable in their fatigue. There were some of us that were told that we could fly away, if we really wanted to. Not everyone had been told that, but I'm sure just about everyone wanted to take flight. I know that the mother and son across the street wanted to be free. I know that the helper man didn't want to be the helper man forever. The prostitutes that would sluggishly stride the street were probably selling themselves short, but I knew that, they too, wanted to be free. I was lucky because I had many voices telling me that I had wings to fly away to freedom. Not everyone has these voices. In other cases, some people know they could fly away if they wanted, but are too fearful of freedom. What if freedom causes fatigue as well? I wish my neighborhood had more voices, telling people that they could fly. These are still MY people.

The summer had its own sound. It seems like there was always a noise thrashing through the streets. I could close my eyes on the porch, and begin to hear the summer soundtrack. I would hear arguments in the distance, and I would try to stretch my range of hearing. Most of it would come from the section-8 apartment next door. Sometimes hearing other people's quarrels helped me selfishly ignore the ones I had inside me. Cars would accelerate down the street boasting all my favorite songs. Sometimes the bass was so loud that the concrete porch under me would rumble, and the parked cars on the street would emit their burglar alarms. Peace had been stolen. There was almost always a dog barking, a baby crying, or a lawn mower guzzling grass. Many times, after I returned inside my home, the sound track would continue. Gunshots would command a brief silence, and soon after sirens would din and dance in the streets. These were sounds that I became accustomed to. This is the reason why I never sat on the porch too long. The murders would be whispered about, all throughout the city. There was so much violence among fatigued people, and yet no one seemed to care. These are still MY people.

Sitting on the porch authenticated the pigments in my skin. I began to understand the role that society has chosen for me, and that it was quite different from what I wanted my role to be. At first, I would speak of what I saw as if I was not a part of it. I had disassociated myself from the neighborhood, because I felt like the anomaly. But after all I had witnessed, I could never disown my porch, or the things it allowed me to see. I couldn't disown the noises, the words, the hunts, or the dilemmas of the neighborhood folk. They are all apart of who I am, and these are still MY people.

A few years later, I was able to "escape" my neighborhood and go on to college.

Houston, Texas

I stepped onto red soil with clenched concrete jungle jaws and pounding orphaned heart. I began my aimless wander. I wasn't ready to trust the smile on my own face. Wasn't ready to trust hospitality.

The sun harassed my skin, following me everywhere. Overtime, we fell in love. I never expected to love something that constantly tested my boundaries. God and the sun have a lot in common.

I marched in the parade on campus every day, trying to find my pace. I began to trust smiles, and I tried to lure them with my own. All these faces were fermenting in the heat, finding their pace in the parade. A few of these faces became familiar. A few of those familiar faces managed to vandalize my smile. Sometimes I found myself in the trenches of betrayal.

I clenched my concrete jungle jaws.

I came here to make my mind into a painting. Something that could ornament a gallery, or two. I carried my canvas like a chip on my shoulder. I had four years to make it a masterpiece. I found my paint in classrooms, in tutoring, in 2am conversations, in bedsheets, in drunken stupor and thrashing music. I found paint spewing from the lips of my shrink, my pastor, and my parents. I found paint, even in my own tears. Everyone was painting, finding their pace in the parade. A lot of the time, I wanted to run back home. Home had faded out of existence.

I clenched my concrete jungle jaws.

I can remember seeing the graffiti "BE SOMEONE" over the I-10 highway. For a long time, it was easier for me to be anyone except myself. But I came here to make my brain a painting. I knew all the color wouldn't come from campus. I needed a village. I needed tribal markings on my face to scare the loneliness away.

Love came to me like mosquitos. It got what it wanted and left. Leaving me with an itch that persisted.

Illness came to me in the form of my shadow. It followed me everywhere I tried to run. Luckily it left me after much time passed.

Wisdom came to me like thorns at my side. Necessary evils that clung to me, and left me with battle scars. Knowledge.

Friendships came to me like plants. I knew they would grow if I watered them. If they died despite my watering, they were never meant to be.

I came to myself. Time and trial brought me the paint that I needed to create my masterpiece.

My masterpiece was born from the parade, from the village and from the *unclenching* of my concrete jungle jaws.

3. The Slavery of Manhood

Toxic Masculinity

What exactly is toxic masculinity? It is unclear where it originates, as many of its components have been reinforced by religion, government, and the patriarchal, capitalist structures of society.

Boys are raised to believe that true manhood lies in the ability to suppress all emotion outside of anger. We have been robbed of the natural human experience. Vulnerability, affection, fear, grief, and even contentment are reserved for women. The concept of assigning emotions to gender is reductive and unrealistic, but this concept is reinforced throughout childhood and into adulthood.

The perils of hyper masculinity, however, affect both genders. Our women are abused, disrespected, harassed, devalued, and degraded because hypermasculinity tells men that it's the "manly" thing to do. It forces us to overcompensate our roles in society and rehearse dominance that, in most cases, isn't even necessary.

You'll witness it in its purest forms:

A man viciously catcalling a woman passing by in order to impress his friends.

A man imploding and forcing himself to hold back tears at his own mother's funeral, because men can't cry.

A man attacking another queer[1] man because he is uncomfortable witnessing someone else flourish in the fluidity of masculinity.

The pressures of hegemonic masculinity appear to correlate with higher suicide rates for men. According to a study on masculinity conducted by C.A.L.M. (Campaign Against Living Miserably), 42% of the men sampled felt that it was necessary for them to be the primary source of income for their household (almost 30% higher than the amount of women who subscribed

---

[1] Similar to African Americans reclaiming the word "nigga", the LGBTQ have reclaimed the word "queer". It is used WITHIN the community as an "umbrella" label to affirm that a person is not cisgendered and/or heterosexual.

to the same belief). 29% of men felt that their partners would see them as less of a man if they lost their job. Within the lens of relationships, around 3 in 10 men believe that they personally lack the qualities or capabilities associated with the sexual/romantic satisfaction that partners look for in a man. 2/3^{rds} of the total sample believed that men are stereotyped within the media.

These social pressures are reinforced by our patriarchal systems, leaving men to internalize depression, anxiety, or feelings of inferiority. The ongoing absence of mental health can drive men to want to take their own life:

"Men were most likely to say they didn't speak to anyone about their depression because they prefer to deal with problems themselves (69%) or because they didn't want to burden people/waste others time (56%)." (Welford and Powell 2014)

But you'll also witness toxic masculinity in the subtle decisions that some men make on a daily basis.

Are you comfortable enough in your manhood to wear that pink shirt? Do you whisper your complex and unbelievably specific order to the barista at Starbucks (do you not want people to know how particular you are about your coffee?) Do you resent your manager at work simply because she's a woman? What about the grunt game? There's always that man in the gym that emits a disturbing declaration of testosterone after that last rep, to let everyone know that he is capable. How open are you with your partner during pillow talks? Does he or she always have to pry it out of you?

God forbid a man doesn't identify with the laws of gender normativity. He'll be called "soft" or "gay" or "girly". These labels echoed in my ears throughout my childhood as I expressed interest in writing, arts, and fashion. Parents often pressure their children to cling to the stereotypical behaviors/interests of their gender. Imagine a young boy who likes the color pink or Barbie dolls. Most men would feel the need to "persuade" or even force their son to abandon expressions of non-stereotypical boyhood. The majority of our attitudes towards our own gender are ingrained into us from toddler years. Perhaps it would be more beneficial to allow the child to discover which gender they identify with the most naturally, instead of coercing them to cooperate within restrictive margins. If a child truly identifies more with the opposite gender, there is nothing the parent can do to change it. In our efforts to police our child's gender performance, we end up causing them a lot of pain and insecurity later on in life. When I look back on my own childhood, I can distinctly remember abandoning some of the activities I loved because I found out that those activities were "designated" for girls. In the same fashion, I often forced myself to entertain other activities that were encouraged for boys. Childhood and adolescence are the most notable periods of self-discovery. Imagine if a child could flourish in whatever form of boyhood/girlhood they please, without feeling the need to adapt.

Most heterosexual men are against having a queer son. Plain and simple. Their son's sexuality appears to reflect on their masculinity; "if my son is gay, that means I've failed as a father. If I've failed as a father, that means I've failed as a man". Aside from religion, I believe that this is the second most common reason that men reject their son's queerness. When I came out to my father, I was worried that he would blame himself, or question his own fatherhood. I wanted him to understand that he did not cause my sexuality. If anything, he was one of the people in my life that pushed me to stay true to myself, and to be a leader. Will my dad go yelling from the mountains that his son is queer? Probably not. But my sexuality doesn't make him love me any less. His affirmation made it easier for me to abandon toxic masculinity.

. The pressures of toxic masculinity are emphasized further more within the African American community. During slavery, black men were stripped of their power and autonomy, creating an insatiable thirst to reclaim it throughout the years since. Even today, as black men struggle to thrive in an arena of systematic racism, clinging to anything that feels like power is comforting. Unfortunately, you will see black men who embody all the qualities of faux-manhood, yet are inactive in their communities, inactive in their families, and inactive in their own development. Amidst the impositions of racial prejudice, there is contrast; black men are valued for their athleticism. We are fetishized because of assumptions about our virility. We somehow become valuable when we are throwing a football or helping a middle aged woman who is bored in her marriage. If young black boys have nothing else to cling to (i.e. education, artistry, etc.), they will only see power in being a tool.

The Barbershop:

For a black man, the barbershop is an experience beyond the haircut. The barbershop serves as a catalyst for dialogue, if nothing else. Because this space is typically absent of women, men have the opportunity to remove most of their layers. Single women sometimes bring their sons in for haircuts at my barbershop, but they often leave their sons and come back to pick them up later. It is quite normal to visit the same barber, in the same barbershop (and inherently abnormal to do otherwise in the black community). In addition to barber loyalty, I suspect that many men return to the same barbershop because they begin to value the platonic relationships that they form with other men. Many men might feel uncomfortable admitting it, but there is a level of vulnerability that occurs in the barbershop that allows us to unload. We talk about our jobs, our relationship problems, our financial struggles, or random experiences that make for great stories.

If I'm not engaging in conversation with my barber, I am eavesdropping on the other conversations that are taking place around me. I don't have to stretch my hearing, because you'll often find these conversations at a dramatic volume, almost commanding your attention. I witness men confiding in each other, actively listening and reinforcing one another's decisions. For that amount of time that you spend waiting on and receiving your haircut, you can let your guard down in a familiar environment. Watching the men in my barbershop interact makes me reflect on my own manhood. It's reassuring to witness proof that the most rugged black men have room in their spirits for vulnerability and love towards other men.

But in the same breath, I'd say that the barbershop can also often be an environment that perpetuates homophobia and misogyny. I've heard conversations about "fruitcakes" and "bitches". Many of my associates who are openly gay and feminine, experience anxiety when they enter the barbershop. The men inside might stare and chuckle, because an openly queer male has entered their space and somehow threatens their manhood. Why can't a queer black man escape being ostracized for an hour and find acceptance among his hetero black counterparts? Why can't men have conversations about women without name calling or implications of sexually assaulting them?

The barbershop is an important part of our community, but it has potential to be greater. I would love to see the hypermasculinity shift into healthy masculinity. The space should be open and accommodating of all men, and respectful to women. My barbershop actively prohibits profanity (because of the children), and saggy pants. I support these rules, but I would also love to see a space that's more inclusive (it's better for business anyway).

Do Black Men Have Daddy Issues?

Daddy issues. Surely, this is a concept we typically use to decorate a woman's emotional voids. It provides plausible context for her decision to be sexually liberated or for her to pursue relationships with men who exceed her in age. Although we assign "daddy issues" to women, we must consider the notion that a great amount of men have "daddy issues" as well. How do males manage the absence of a positive male role model in their lives? The most common response is internalization, followed by implosion.

Not having a blueprint for true manhood leaves a lot of room for young men to entertain self-neglecting concepts of masculinity. They have no recipe for manhood, so they have to make it from scratch. They pull ingredients from their coach, or from the streets, or from their church, or maybe from nowhere. Of course, I myself have been tempted to adapt faux-manhood. Although not nearly genuine, it's the quickest way to feel like you have that power that I mentioned earlier. It's enticing to use it as leverage against your own insecurities.

Growing up, I often felt abnormal for having an active father in my life. Many of my peers had limited or no contact with their fathers, and I witnessed them demonstrate their hurt in different ways. Some seemed to bask in their feelings of inferiority, refusing to apply themselves in school. Others would fold into themselves emotionally, building up walls in effort to prevent additional disappointment. I saw some of my peers seek love in the streets (most people don't realize that a lot of gang members are looking for a sense of family or protection). If this security isn't present in the child's household they will begin to seek these elements elsewhere. My father did not have a father growing up, and he did the best he could raising me. Although there were a few gaps, his presence in my life was invaluable and crucial for my growth.

One thing holds to be true: there is hope for all men to learn true manhood. Boys without fathers or positive male role models don't have to grow up into self-loathing, aggressive, emotionally unavailable tyrants. You cannot spend your whole life holding your breath. It's OK to have weak moments. It's OK to rely on others for support. It's OK to be opinionated and emotionally intelligent. If you have pain that you are hiding away, you will never heal. You will become a threat to yourself, and to the people closest to you. We are not designed to be superheroes, despite what the rest of the world foolhardily expects of us.

We should aim to abandon hyper masculine tendencies and begin to nurture our young boys more. If they express interest in painting, or dancing, or baking, we should encourage them to enjoy those activities. Boys should be taught to be more expressive and open about their feelings, so that they will not develop a habit of bottling them. Respect for women should be both taught and demonstrated. Black boys come into the world with a variety of pressures; it's our responsibility to remove the pressure of faux-manhood from them. Lead by example, and reconsider what "manning up" means to you.

Be a hero to yourself, and flourish in your own space of manhood.

Flower Boy

There was this man I met eyes with
On 95th
Dressed to suppress himself
His demeanor was like a song I knew all the words to
I hear it everywhere

He was wearing his manhood like a helmet
Just in case he ran into freedom

He saw me
Drenched in apprehensive sweat
Wearing my freedom like a helmet
Just in case I ran into intolerance

Our exchange in glances was conversational
For a moment, I saw flowers in his eyes
They had been watered by his tears
And he was no longer as threatening as he appeared

He needed healing, but nobody else knew it
He had everyone around him fooled
But I saw right through it

For a moment, he dropped his performance
He became a boy playing in a safe place
For a moment, I saw my reflection

We were both stricken
Oppression helped us love each other
I told him, it was ok to be a flower
He told me, it was ok to like them

Eclipse

If you catch a man unloading
You have witnessed an eclipse
Vulnerability that manifests every few years or so
And only lasts for minutes

All the time in between you'll find him
Dancing barefoot on broken glass
Boldly professing how he doesn't need shoes
Or how his steps are only rite of passage
In becoming a man

Men abandon themselves
In search of manhood
And we find their carcasses, still dancing
Dead inside, yet living to dance
Living to perform

To my fellow man
We all find ourselves dancing on broken glass
But the next time someone offers you shoes
You should take them
Every eclipse is beautiful.

Hypermasculinity Haikus

(because men love keeping shit short)

What are you wearing?
Boy, pick a different color
Pink is for pussies

I hate Beyoncé
Unless I'm all by myself
Don't tell anyone

This is a man's world
Everything would be better
Without a woman

My dad wasn't there
So I pretend not to care
If it feels like love

Ego is counting
Hairs on another man's head
I think I am God

Loving to my mom
I am misogynistic
How can I be both?

I'm not a hero
I wear manhood like a cape
It makes me feel safe

I'll find brotherhood
Even if I lose my life
I'll have a family

Manhood is an act
Don't blame me for forgetting
Remind me my lines

Before I admit
I need to confide in you
I will make you pry

I am a straight male
I don't like feminine men
Their lives affect mine

I am a straight male
And I cannot accept love
From another man

Fence

Boy can't pick a side
Boy is told until he can pick one,
He has to hide.

Can't take shelter in a woman's arms
Unless he plans to stay
Can't take shelter in a man's arms
Without being called gay

Boy can't pick a side
Boy doesn't really have to
The world has picked it for him
And whatever side of the fence the boy gets pushed to
There's nobody around to support him

Boy is told to be true to himself
As long as his truth can be
Approved by someone else

So now he has to pick
Red lips and wide hips, or
A soldier with broad shoulders

Boy can't pick a side
Spends his life wondering if
He's on the right one
And he hasn't even picked yet.

Chest Hairs

Be a man they said
And thus my search began

Manhood was good with his hands
Manhood built levees into my eyelids
So the hairs on my cheeks could grow
Like cactuses that didn't need much water

Manhood was the Equator
You're getting warmer...warmer it said
If you want to get warmer, you gotta get colder

Manhood came to me
In the form of a jail cell
My crimes were in my voice, my glitter,
My locking of eyes in locker rooms

Manhood came to me
In the form of freedom
In swinging breasts that said *look but don't touch*
Manhood came to me in
Shoulder taps and fist bumps and head nods
These are the limits of our love it said

Manhood clung to me
Like tank top cotton on my sweaty back
Manhood was one continuous church hug to myself

Somewhere along the way
Manhood became a revolution
When manhood no longer meant
Manhandling my own heart
Manhood came to me

45

4. 3 Minutes Into A Mental Breakdown

Rock Bottom

The most challenging part of my life thus far was the majority of my undergraduate career. Navigating the labyrinths of postsecondary education can be enough to drive anyone into a depressive state. I watched my peers tackle an array of different "slaps in the face". As humans, there are many challenges that we share, and we develop algorithms for overcoming them. But sometimes, we are faced with situations that leave us at wit's end; situations that strip us of our emotional, mental, and even physical fortitude.

I spent the majority of my college years knowing that I wasn't truly happy. I became a professional in "displaying" happiness on my social media, or rehearsing it during my daily interactions, but those quiet moments I had with myself would always be the clearest moments. In my situation, I knew exactly what was ailing me, I just had no idea how to remedy it. Ever heard *"Cranes in the Sky"* by Solange?

During my freshman year, towards the end of my first semester, I began to get sick. I found myself consistently nauseous, with weakness, headaches, chest pain, and racing heartrate. There were some days that I would get a full 8 hours of rest the night before, take a 2 hour midday nap, and still be exhausted. Because I couldn't eat often, I was losing weight, and began to feel even worse. It became challenging to apply myself in my classes, because I was feeling ill 80% of the time. The pressure of failing my classes and disappointing everyone who invested time and money into me was eating me alive. God knows that at that time, I didn't even want to fathom being a disappointment to anyone. I had run away from my hometown Chicago down to Houston, a completely different environment. I was miles away from home, and learning how to take care of myself was a daunting process.

My issues with my stomach began to worsen. There were days where I'd stay home because of the fear of throwing up in class. Upon trying natural remedies and OTC medicine I was still doubled over in my dorm room with ongoing discomfort. I began to isolate myself from my friends, because being social quickly became a chore for me.

After I returned home for my first Christmas break, I finally had time to visit a doctor. My doctor initially gambled that my illness was related to anxiety. I can remember feeling furious about her conclusion. Basic blood testing didn't reveal anything more than a couple vitamin deficiencies, and this was probably a result of not eating. The search would continue for me to find out what was going on.

My first winter break back home was the most restorative; I was beyond ready to be back in a familiar space (although many things had changed since I had left for college). I actually missed my parents, and delighted in the care they gave me as I attempted to recover from my illness. I took comfort in assuming that once this "thing" ran its course, I could return to my normal life. I had no idea that this was only a taste of the sickness that would follow.

I returned to school with intent, taking pride in knowing that I had survived my first semester of college, despite all the demons that tried to destroy me. I found it difficult to open up to my friends about my illness, especially since I still didn't have a diagnosis. Still, I felt obligated to provide an explanation for my lack of interest in social activities. "I've been sick, I have stomach issues" would be my curt explanation when asked about my recent whereabouts. I would try to avoid going into more detail, and would often deflect with statements about how concerned I was with my grades. "Oh, yea, I've been studying a lot, I just want to get a head start for the semester, you know?"

Eventually, my friends accepted my reclusive nature. The random door knocks and Facetime calls halted, and I found myself feeling guilty, as if I had failed them. The copious amount of time I spent in solitude allowed me to reflect on the dissatisfaction with my own life. College quickly became a burden for me, as it meant that I had to constantly balance my academic curriculum with my painful transition into adulthood.

As time went on, my stomach issues persisted. Finishing my second semester, I had inadvertently developed a tolerance for my illness. By "tolerance" I mean that my illness became a part of my life, like a new abusive relationship. However, my lack of health began to affect my mental health as well. Depression was beginning to impact many facets of my life. I knew that I needed to return to the doctor and look for answers, because despite my "tolerance", my patience was wearing thin. Upon returning home to Chicago for summer break, I began an exhausting tour of the medical process. Before I even reached the doctor's office, I would have to familiarize myself with my insurance. I researched how to articulate my symptoms effectively to the doctor, so that I could get answers fast (to no avail). I prepared myself to receive life altering news (can you really prepare yourself for that?). Upon arriving at the doctor's office, I would embark on a journey of frustration. If I had a nickel for every time I was poked with a needle for a blood test, I would have enough money to buy a nice book. I am referring to a coffee table book, not a book for a college class. There are not enough nickels in circulation for that.

The blood tests would come back negative or normal, except for the occasional low iron or Vitamin-D. I can remember the disappointment I felt every time I received "normal" results on my blood tests. This meant that whatever was wrong with me was either all in my head, or sneaky enough to evade detection via blood. But when the blood tests couldn't deliver answers, the noninvasive and invasive testing eventually began.

Before that fun stuff, I went back to college for my sophomore year with no answers. By this time, I had seen a general doctor in both Houston and Chicago. I would sit across from the doctors, who initially discredited the possibility of me having a serious disease, based on my age. Eventually, I realized that seeing a specialist was my best chance of getting a proper diagnosis. I had finally made my way into a gastroenterologist's office in Chicago during spring break, and I can remember him telling me to try cutting gluten from my diet for 4 weeks. Once I found out what gluten consisted of, and what I had to eliminate from my diet, I laughed in disbelief. Prior to that point, I had no clue what gluten[2] was, and couldn't imagine myself being sensitive or allergic to it. But I decided to humor my doctor and try it out.

After about 2 weeks, I began to feel a lot better. I noticed that my stomach was upset less often, and I was able to eat more. The headaches and dizziness improved, as well as the fatigue. So was that it? I could never eat gluten again? This would definitely be a painful adjustment to my diet, as many of the foods that I used to fill the voids of college angst were stuffed with gluten. Shit. The first world voice inside me screamed out: "Is life even worth living if I can't eat a 6 pack of birthday cupcakes from Walmart?"

---

[2] Gluten refers to the group of proteins that are found in wheat, barley, and rye. When embarking on a miserable gluten free diet, the obvious no-no's are cereal, bread, pasta, and baked goods. But because gluten is present in normal flour, it is often present in soups, sauces, fried foods, certain candies, dressings, and much more.

I gradually adjusted into a gluten free diet and life was normal for about a month. After that month, my symptoms returned. Only now, whenever I would consume gluten by mistake, I would get very sick. I realized that I probably needed to find a GI (gastroenterologist) doctor in Houston, because that was where I spent most of my year. If this was an ongoing issue, I would need to have access to a good doctor in both cities.

My GI doctor in Houston was a godsend. She was passionate about her patients and she committed herself to helping me get to the root of my issues. She was unconcerned about blood tests. She was adamant about taking a look at my GI system, and immediately scheduled me for a series of tests. I can remember doing ultrasounds on my organs. I can remember the procedure in which I had to drink a huge container of barium and take X-rays as it moved through my system. Conceptually it was cool, but I wanted to puke the whole time. I even got to swallow a techy camera pill that allowed the doctor to capture images of my insides. She saw inflammation in my stomach and small intestine and decided that she wanted to do an endoscopy. This procedure meant that they would be putting me to sleep and jamming (I'm being dramatic) a long scope down my throat. I had never had a procedure with anesthesia before and I can remember being anxious about it. The desperation for answers and diagnosis allowed me to swallow my anxiety (and the scope). Upon waking from the procedure, the doctor told me that she had found inflammation and ulcers in my duodenum and small intestine. She was beginning to suspect that I had Crohn's disease. She wanted to conduct a colonoscopy to examine the "other end" of my GI tract, but the school year was coming to a close. We arranged to have a colonoscopy with my doctor in Chicago, and I would send her the results so that she could confirm or deny the disease. I returned home, anxious again to lie on an operating table as a scope was jammed into my butt. Just in case you're reading this book during your cozy lunch, I won't spoil it with the details of preparation for a colonoscopy procedure. Wild.

Upon completion of this procedure, they also discovered similar inflammation and ulceration in my large intestine. My doctor in Houston was hesitant to place me on drug therapy for Crohn's because she still wasn't entirely sure if that was the answer. Instead, she placed me on a relatively strong anti-inflammatory for the GI tract. Pentasa. I had to take this pill four times a day, along with a daily acid reducer. I prayed that the medication would work and that I would be able to return to a normal life.

Trapped:

On top of my ongoing health issues, I was also the victim of my own self-hatred. The other exhausting crusade of my college career was hiding my sexuality. I was raised in a densely Christian household, and was told that homosexuality was an abomination. I couldn't admit to anyone around me that I was queer, because for the longest I couldn't even admit it to myself. I prided myself in my faux-masculinity, and embraced the rumors of being a womanizer that followed me on campus. At that point in my life, I was more proud to be the hyper masculine, womanizer instead of being proud of my actual self. My desire to mask my sexuality dictated many aspects of my life; I did not realize how much effort I was putting into this ruse. I was so uncomfortable in my own skin that I often left it in the hands of others. I was certain that the people around me would reject my sexuality and judge me without hesitation.

Many of the people in my life couldn't identify with my struggles around my health or my sexuality. They could only offer encouragement and a listening ear.

Of course I was grateful for the support I had, but the feelings of isolation and loneliness began to dominate me. I felt that most of my relationships were superficial, and I tried to force myself to be content with that. I don't care what anyone says, being trade[3] is not fun. I couldn't trust the validity of the relationships I had, because very few people knew me entirely.

Being sick made it easier for me to hide myself away from who I wanted to be. I often envisioned myself coming out to my friends and family, flourishing in my truth. It seemed like a distant fantasy. At that toxic time, masking myself and living to appease others seemed more realistic.

For the longest, I felt like I had to choose between my sexuality and my religion. I had been told that God hated gays, and I began to hate myself. During undergrad, hiding my sexuality allowed me to feel safe, knowing that no one could reject me for that aspect of my life. However, I was miserable, because many of my relationships were bland. I felt extremely isolated because no one knew me beyond my barriers. I feared that women would reject a bi man, and that my straight male friends wouldn't want to be around one. I feared

---

[3] Trade refers to a man who is secretly attracted to other men, or down-low. Most people assume that he is heterosexual and would be shocked to find out that he was queer.

that I would lose friendships, or that my reputation on campus would be tainted. I feared that people would see my sexuality before they saw the rest of me, and that I would have to carry my label like a scarlet letter. But during my sophomore year, I built up the courage to tell one of my family members. We were very close and I decided that I no longer wanted to hide that aspect of my life from them. I've decided to keep their identity protected, for deference.

As I stumbled through my words and trembled in my chair, I had no idea that coming out to this person would change our relationship forever.

"I'm bisexual"

In that moment, I wasn't just admitting it to them, I was admitting it to myself. It was real now. I broke down in tears because I felt it coming. This was a pivotal moment in my life, because this was the first time that my fear of rejection had materialized right before my eyes. I was far more impressionable at that point in my life, so the homophobia and intolerance hurt me to the core. This person asked me "what are we going to do to fix it?" "Do you think it's just a phase?" "Have you prayed for God to remove that desire from your heart?" I felt this person trying to talk me out of my reality. I wanted to run as far away from them as I could, and luckily I only had to wait another day to return to campus. I can remember crying on the Megabus back to Houston, because I have never allowed myself to cry in a public place (aside from childhood). I felt so damaged and guilty, but most of all, like I had failed this person. The thought of experiencing this rejection and intolerance from friends and other family terrified me. I wanted to cower into the façade of my hetero lifestyle and never emerge from it again.

I spent months arguing with this person. Trying to help them understand my dilemma and my perspective. I wanted them to grasp the notion that I wasn't choosing to be this way. It wasn't a life decision. Let's be honest, who would choose to be queer in a world full of hatred and homophobia? The arguments turned into distance, and the distance turned into me trying to convince myself that I was worthy of more love than that. I was worried that this person would tell the rest of the family, and then I would be rejected by multiple people. It wasn't until my senior year of undergrad that I developed the courage to tell another friend or family member.

Sometimes, I pondered ending my life. Between my health and battling with my identity, I was unsure if I'd ever be happy. At the beginning of my senior year, I was at rock bottom.

My illness had left me thin and weak. My medication wasn't working, but the side effects were working overtime. I had been taking the Pentasa for a few months now, but I was still having bad flare ups. I would show up to the dining hall, swipe in, and leave 5 minutes later because I was too nauseous to eat anything. I would carry around Zofran in my wallet. Zofran is an antiemetic that dissolves on your tongue. During my rough flare ups, I would be taking them almost daily. I had no energy to study, let alone socialize or date. Almost every night, I would wake up from my sleep sweating and nauseous. I would leave my bed in the morning, still fatigued; pushing myself to get through the day. I can remember praying in the shower and asking God: "if you could just get me through this day, I'll figure the rest out later". I was always dizzy, or faint, or wincing in discomfort. Eventually, I began to lose sight of my future, because the present was too demanding of my attention. I wanted to secure a job for graduation, but I hadn't heard from the company I was applying for. I would show up everywhere with the intent of leaving early. Work, class, bible study, you name it. I didn't want to be anywhere but in my room. It was bad enough that my illness was a nuisance to me, but the thought of it being a nuisance to other people made me cringe. I fought my way through my course load because I was determined not to fail. Aside from this effort, I was dead on the inside. I was tired of spending money on medical bills and medicine that wasn't helping me feel better. I was tired of feeling distant from my own body; the ambiguity of my illness was mentally draining. My friends and family watched me deteriorate into a lifeless marionette. I found myself at church, Bible study, and counseling trying to cram all the positivity into my mind that I could. I pondered if life was really worth living. I wanted to take my own life, and there was one night that I seriously considered it. I had a handful of Tylenol 3 pills and I pondered. I thought about the people that would be hurt. I thought about the potential that I would lose. I thought about hell. But in my mind, I was already in hell on earth. I really pondered. I hated my condition, my sexuality, my generic off-brand relationships, my insecurities. They all became whispers in my ear telling me that dying would be better. But as I made my final deliberations, I heard a voice as clear as day say to me, "Just hold on a little bit longer." I knew it wasn't the voice in my head, because that voice was telling me to eat the pills. It had to be God himself. I couldn't ignore the voice, and I quickly snapped out of my pondering. Sometimes I wonder what would have happened if that voice didn't come to me.

3 days later, I got a call from the company I had been yearning to work for. They extended a job offer. I was relieved that I would have a position in my field after graduation, and certain that all my hard work had paid off. I knew then that God was going to take care of the rest. I figured that there was no way He'd give me this huge opportunity if I was going to be suffering forever.

From this moment in November, right before Thanksgiving, my life gradually started to improve. My medication was finally beginning to relieve my symptoms, and after Christmas break, I was beginning to feel healthy again. I was starting to gain my weight back, and was able to enjoy eating most of the time. During the time before December, I was feeling ill 80% of the time. By March of the next year, I was only feeling ill 20% of the time. Although my GI doctor suspected that I had Crohn's disease, we were never able to completely confirm the condition. Regardless, the symptoms were starting to fade. Quite naturally, the progression of my physical health aided the progression of my mental health as well. My depression and anxiety became manageable, and as graduation approached, I wanted to give coming out another chance. I realized that I would never be happy if I couldn't be myself. I needed to know who would love me regardless of my identity. I became less fearful of rejection because I wanted to surround myself with people who knew me in totality and loved me the same.

By no means was it easy to begin the journey. However, as I began to tell my friends, they would reinforce me and tell me that I was silly for hiding it from them. Most of the women whom I had dated in the past were unbothered by my bisexuality and embraced it. My straight male friends were receptive and challenged themselves to understand my world. I felt like I was finally standing on solid ground. Slowly but surely, I was building up the bravery to tell my parents, and the rest of my family. I decided I would wait until after graduation, because I didn't want any drama to ruin my day.

I worked my ass off for that degree, and I needed everyone to be fully engaged as I walked across that stage.

But anywho, I was finding my way to freedom. I talked to God about my decisions and asked to Him to guide me as I had these conversations with family. I asked Him to help me remain calm and realistic. During the summer after graduation (literally last summer), I told my nephew, cousins, mother, father, and aunts that I was bi. As you can imagine, the reactions varied. As much as I want to regret coming out, I can't. I know that I am truly happier now because of my honesty with myself and the people I cherish. Have I subjected myself to discrimination and bigotry? Yes. Will it defeat me? No. I now have multiple people in my life who are beyond supportive of my identity, and that is one of the most gratifying feelings. 4 years ago, I would have never imagined to be open about my sexuality, let alone writing about it in my book. I am proud of the progression and growth. I am proud of me now.

None of this would be possible without self-love. It's a process that takes time to master. If you don't find self love in this life, you'll never be truly happy.

Anxiety's Scavenger Hunt

Fight or flight
Has my heartrate soaring over safety
No rational thought in sight
Worry has left me trying to find boundaries in my breath

Stumbling into thoughts in my mind that
I was never supposed to find
Still searching for the sense in the two cents my shrink
gave me
Still don't have enough to buy a sound mind

But you can catch me running through fields
Trying to find a reason to keep breathin'
Trying to outrun the demons

Took drugs so I could function
But what if drugs took me instead?
What if I can't find homeostasis?
What if I lose this scavenger hunt?

If I drink so I can think straight,
And die from being too high
Would that be called a "liver failure?"

I keep telling myself that I'll be alright
It's hard to trust someone that you don't know
I want to reach for something that'll end this hunt
Because most of the time
I don't even know what I'm looking for

Wilting

They call me
Peculiar flower
Trying to thrive in darkness

Pushed its way through
The dirt everyone wants to wash away
Reaching toward distant sun

Father, I stretch my hands to Thee
For my roots no longer want to claim me
Here I stand
Wilting
Because I thought I found my home in homelessness

Wilting
Because I've only been watered
With yesterday's tears
I told myself I wouldn't cry anymore
Even if it killed me

I told myself that eventually
A gardener will stop by and remember
That despite my wilting
I am still a flower

A few of my pedals
Are still wealthy in color
My roots pick and choose
Which parts of me they want to claim
I'm wilting
Because it doesn't work that way

Father, I stretch my hands to Thee
Because you are the everlasting sun
And you don't have
Favorite flowers

Burnt Down

I sway
With shadows shivering on my skin
As I watch my own home
Burn to the ground

I fought my way
Through smoke and soot
Only to realize that I abandoned
My only refuge

I thought I needed air
But I can hear my family
Screaming for me inside the house
I whisper uncertain "goodbyes"

I can feel the heat
Gently caressing my face
And it's telling me that I should have stayed
As if I was furnace coal

I stand here wishing
That I couldn't hear sirens in the distance
I survived the fire
But there's nothing that can save me
Now that I'm outside

Trees

They say never take shelter under a tree
When it's lightening
But how do trees take shelter?
Being firmly rooted doesn't make you suited
To stand the storm
Having branches that move with the wind
Won't stop them from being blown away

And yet when a storm comes
Instead of leaving, the tree has to stay

What if I'm the tree?
What if I'm expected to withstand the pain?
When everyone else seems to evade the rain

What if, in all its absurdity, being a tree
Is somehow worth it,
Because you'll be the first to see the sun after the storm
And know that you deserve it.

Body

Truly to'up from the flo up
My feet are planted down on the most
Unstable ground
My knees buckle from the breeze and
I am anxious for a Langston to define my "Hughes"

Because without knowledge, I only have legs to stand on.
And my third leg is busy
Craving a southern belle from Mississippi
Or maybe New Orleans
My hips should've been whipped a
Little harder by momma
Her voice resounds even in the loudest of crowds

My stomach is the tightest knot I know
I'm holding on to breakfast but
I might have to let it go.
There are a thousand sorrows burning
In my gut
The bad news that is ingested
But cannot be digested
Sometimes my chest forgets how
To accommodate breath and I find
Myself gasping
Or sometimes I find myself puffing
Or sometimes I find myself relying
On the hope of dying

My heart is a woman in constant labor
Pushing life into a child
In hopes that it'll all be worth while
My arms tell stories that my mouth
Can't verbalize
My fists are balled and ready
For any creature that may crawl
Over my tall walls and try to

Love me

My mouth is the elephant in the room

If I'm stressed, I'll press upon the bladder
Of the matter no one wants to address
Until your pants are wet.
And now you're a scared child just like me

My eyes have seen history in rehabilitation
"Hello, my name is History and I am addicted
To repeating myself"
Every time I look for the good in life
I go blind and commit a crime
My brain is shot
Each corner of my mind is in desperate
Search of another corner of its own kind
So yea, a whole lotta' dead ends

But no split ends
Because my hair is flowing in the promise of warmer
winds
Maybe it's not as stiff and dead
As everything below the top of my head..

Storm Chasing

I see my dream
Just beyond the static
Waving its finger in my face
And telling me to grab it

I'm too tired to run
And I'm too rushed to stroll
So I'm stuck skipping along
As if I am merry and whole

I wish I could fumble through the fog
And find comfort in its form
If only I could find love
In the heart of the storm

But here I am
Just a few steps behind
And every step I take
Seems like a waste of time

5. Return to Sender

Self Love

A couple of years ago, I thought self-love was a façade. How often do you hear men talk about self-love openly? I didn't see it as actionable or ritualistic, and definitely didn't deem myself worthy of it. As a black man, I rarely witnessed other men in my community prioritizing mental health. Some men would even boast about self-neglect, as if it was a pillar of true manhood. I struggled with the concept of self-acceptance, and self-love was at the bottom of my "to-do" list. I exhausted all my love in meeting expectations. I loved what others wanted me to be, and focused on making my performance seamless. At that point, self-love was like winning the lottery; I knew others would win it, but I didn't think I had chances of winning it myself. Even in my own skin, it was difficult to understand my heart and my spirit. I couldn't fathom being able to love myself beyond the language barriers. How could someone trust self-love when the "self" has so much volatility? The task seemed daunting, and it was probably easier for me to approach it with skepticism, or not approach it at all.

I'd be lying if I said that I am certain about when I began to practice self-love (or when I began to even acknowledge it as a practice). Maybe it was being surrounded by so many people who reinforced the real "me". Maybe it was realizing that I would never be satisfied attempting to satisfy others. Maybe it was God, or a combination of all these things. However, I know for certain that it wasn't an immediate transition. I think that much like martial arts, we all have to start as white belts. Being a "white belt" in self-love means that someone can come along and knock you on your back with ease. If you keep rising and fighting, eventually you'll look around and realize that you are a black belt. It takes time and effort to stand firmly and unapologetically; self-love is a struggle.

One of my biggest hurdles was seeking validation. Seeking validation from other people around me was a result of me placing so much value on their opinions. I would constantly try to convince myself that other people's opinions didn't matter, because I wanted to be able to live my life without asking society's permission. However, it seemed futile, because I would often end up feeling like a passenger in my own life. What I felt was popular or socially acceptable had its hands on the wheel.

College provided me with the space I needed to find self-love. It was like a random encounter with a stranger on the street that turned into a long lasting friendship. As I unraveled with self-neglecting practices and found myself unable to be comfortable in my own skin, it became more apparent that I needed to find a solution for my lack of fortitude. As I watched my friends appear to flourish in their own skin, I became more conscious of my emptiness. I wanted to cling to what the Bible, my parents, peers, and social media told me to be. I felt like a child, constantly looking for guidance from the voices in my head, or the posts in my Twitter feed, or the conversations I would overhear in the Student Center. I was obsessed with obliging many of the extrinsic pressures around me. The start of me loving myself was also the start of me letting these expectations go. "So what if I'm not what you expected me to be? This is not your life!"

I wanted to look in the mirror and be satisfied with what I saw. I had countless mornings before class in which I'd glance into the mirror in my bathroom, teary eyed and cold. But gradually, I began to give myself a chance. I stopped hesitating. I began to wear the clothes that I liked, listen to the music that I identified with, and be more comfortable in my masculinity. I stopped blaming myself for the parts of me that I couldn't control...my history, my race, my sexuality. I stopped policing my personality, and became more authentic in my day-to-day interactions. I felt myself evolving; it was like having a front row seat to one of the best shows of all time. I began to feel myself smile more, not to soothe others, but because I actually wanted to smile. Instead of trying to find my place in the world, I redirected my energy to nurture the world inside me. That way, no matter what happens externally, I would always have a true home.

Have I mastered self-love? No, I am not a black belt quite yet. Can I tell you exactly how to love yourself appropriately? Of course not, self-love looks different for everyone. Some people might need to embark on emotional journeys, or physical journeys, or spiritual journeys. Nevertheless, I can stress the importance of this journey to anyone. It won't be an instant process, and sometimes it will feel hopeless. Despite its initial permeability, time and effort will fill its gaps and reinforce it. Learning who you are and developing a routine for maintaining your peace is important for your survival. Self-love will help you defeat self-doubt, anxiety, depression, and suicidal thoughts. Self-love will allow you to find validation within self, instead of all of the other toxic places we tend to search for it. I'd like to share my routine, because it has been a critical part in my growth.

Day to Day:

1. Daily morning devotion. Talking to a God that loves me perfectly is a great way to learn how to love myself more effectively.

2. Hygiene. Aside from the basics, I somehow manage to jam my excessive hair and skin care routine into my morning ritual.

3. Music. I literally listen to music almost 24 hours of the day. I use it to uplift my spirit and to help me process what I am feeling.

4. 1 Small Gift. Every day, I'll try to give myself a small gift, or treat myself to something nice. This can be anything from grabbing ice cream to watching my favorite show on TV. The whole point is to remind myself that I am worth small gifts.

5. Fashion. I really aim to look my best, even when I am feeling my worst. I take pride in "not

looking like what I'm currently going through"
as my pastor would say. Leaving the house
looking like I'm about to walk down a runway
for NY Fashion week helps me stay confident
and comfortable in my skin. In my head, I'm
just a D-list celebrity that hasn't had their big
break yet.

When Stressed:

1. Late night car rides. My mind tends to race at
    night, and whenever I become overwhelmed
    with negative thoughts, I'll go for a drive.
    Something about driving on the quiet roads in
    the dullness of night is soothing for me.

2. Talking. When I'm highly upset, sometimes my
    first reaction is to internalize it. As I am
    working on divorcing toxic practices of
    masculinity, I challenge myself to talk through
    my problems. I am blessed with friends and
    family who provide listening ears and pats on
    the back, when needed.

3. Writing. Sitting down in a quiet space and
    writing poetry helps bring me back to earth
    when I am feeling upset or feeling down. This

practice also helps me materialize what I am
feeling.

4. Planning. It might sound weird, but whenever
    the present seems unrelenting, I like to plan for
    the future. Maybe subconsciously, I am
    reminding myself that I have one, and that
    whatever I am currently dealing with, will pass.

5. Cooking. I am a self-declared master chef.
    Although I also like to cook when I am not
    stressed, there is something about the stress of
    the kitchen that helps distract me from my other
    dilemmas. In the midst of trying not to burn my
    garlic or overcook my shrimp, I escape my
    overarching stress for a while. Cooking helps
    me feel like I am in control, and at the end, I get
    to enjoy a great meal.

6. Topman. Not sure if this is a healthy practice,
    but it helps to walk into your favorite clothing
    store and purchase new items for your
    wardrobe. This practice supports the Day-to-
    Day fashion practice above.

I don't expect my self-love routine to be completely
relatable, but I find comfort in these practices. I have
become aware of what helps me stay rooted in me (and

my sanity). Life can be hard at times, and not being connected to yourself will make it harder.

I urge people to take time to reconnect with yourself. Challenge yourself to learn what eases your mind and start allocating time for these activities. I can give a few other examples of practices that are common within the realm of self love. But ultimately, the journey is unique for everyone that tackles it.

Physical:

Running/Exercising. Taking a long hot bath or going to a spa. Practicing guided Yoga/Meditation. Learn deep breathing exercises. Eating your favorite meal or going to your favorite restaurant. Changing your hairstyle/color. Taking a vacation. Spending quality time with friends or family. Embarking on a cleanse/detox.

Mental/Emotional:

Seeking therapy (there is nothing wrong with this). Write down the things that you want to let go on paper, then burn it. Write down your goals. Talk to people you trust. Keep a journal. Give yourself accolades for your accomplishments.

Spiritual:

Pray incessantly. Find a church/mosque/temple to attend regularly. If you're not religious, collect some of your favorite inspirational quotes and meditate on them daily. Burn sage (to dispel demons and bad spirits). Remove yourself from negative energy (it can manifest in a person, place, or thing).

I also have to remind myself that I am valid, and that I have value. Being able to leave your home daily knowing that you are loved by yourself and those around you is a great feeling. Being proud of everything that embodies "you" is self-love. Avoiding toxic practices, relationships, and friendships is self-love. Coping and forgiving yourself for your mistakes is self-love. Pulling yourself back from the ledge that life sometimes puts you on is self-love. It is okay if you are a white belt in self-love. You have time to transition, and become someone who can stand boldly and "solely" in their own two shoes.

The poems I have included in this chapter outline my struggles and victories with self-love.

Boxed In

I thought that I could be
More than a suggestion box
In a dim hallway
Outside the door of freedom

The door that glistens
with dandelion and lullabied sun
The door that breathes warm winds
And calls everyone's name but mine

I am filled to the brim
With wishes upon a star
Wishes that I could be
Anything but myself

God please, not myself

I've heard rumors
That I'll never get to unload
The masses of madness inside me
That I'll always be a wooden box

Open only to receive
The damage done by Adam and Eve
Open only through a tiny slot
To take in the narrow thoughts of narrow minded

Open only
To avoid being empty
So that I'll have enough instruction
To be anyone besides myself

God please, not myself

Moving

We all stand
Like apprehensive children
Looking for candy in love's candor

Our hearts follow familiarity
And our hands place cart before horse
Of course, it feels right staying still sometimes,
Because what we know is hard to divorce

Then we find ourselves hitch hiking from
Heartache to heartache
Waiting on maybes and being called crazy
For doing so.

And then we get led to the alter
For alternatives
Still hitch hiking
Still trying to wedge ourselves into the corner
Of the world that feels right
And yet wanting the world to be in our corner

We all stand
Peering over naked shoulder
Looking for a reason to stay

A Letter to My Pastor

Hey Pastor
I'm glad I looked past you and
saw God for myself

I sat before you in full allegiance
Cradled in your conspiracy
Not even realizing that I had become Jonah
Trapped in the belly of self-hatred

Leaving church feeling nourished enough
To starve myself

Hey pastor
I'm so glad God looks past you
And all the damage you do
I'm so glad God didn't forget about Jonah

Tundra

Loving yourself is
Like howling at the moon
Singing to the distant intangible
When the world around you just wants you
To shut up

I hope you aren't taking dirty rags
And trying to wash the purest parts of you away
I hope you know
That your crosshairs are paradoxical

Loving yourself is
Reciting barbed wire around your heart
So the thieves can't steal your peace

I hope you plant evergreen affirmations
In your garden
Words that will outstand the winters
I hope you'll find shelter
After you are exiled

Mirror Boy

Sometimes I can't stand to look at you
But I have to stop by and make sure
You're still there

Don't Break

It doesn't matter
If the glass is half empty
Or half full
If the glass itself
Is broken

6.Forget-Me-Nots

Love

Love is one of the most baffling subjects of
them all. It is sometimes fleeting, and other times long-
lasting. People encounter it unexpectedly, and others go
their whole life searching for it. Much of my perception
on love has been influenced by my parents' relationship.
I watched two very different people express love in their
own ways, and the robust (I choose my words carefully)
nature of my parents' marriage has given me a more
realistic expectation of what love is supposed to be. My
father tends to show love through action, while my mom
is more verbal. Over the years, I've watched them
recalibrate their love languages, ultimately working to
meet each other in the middle. I am proud of them for
surviving the volatility of marriage, because it is far more
common for people to walk away from their
commitments prematurely. Because my parents survived

the challenges of their marriage, I feel like I can approach my relationships with more tact.

Although the majority of my love life is lived vicariously through my friends, I was able to write countless poems about my experiences with it. Despite my hesitation to admit it, I've probably experienced love in a multitude of ways. I've experienced love in gestures, late night conversations, eye contact, arguments, and companionship. Love radiates from me and I, as a man, can acknowledge that. I walk around on this earth willing to give it to the darkest corners.

Love, by no means, is easy. But you have to be clear on what you are willing to tolerate and what you are not. Because I have such a broad understanding of what I am NOT willing to tolerate, I have a pretty intense selection process when it comes to dating. Yes, I'm the picky friend. Yes, I am the person that would rather be alone instead of spending years trying to force someone into the mold of what I expect them to be. If you have a lot to bring to the table, you shouldn't mind eating alone for a while. Love is about compromise, but is not supposed to trap you into misery. That's called settling, just in case you weren't sure. Settling is for lawyers.

Of course, these are only my opinions. But I have dated long enough to know that some situations are dead horses and lost causes. My poems about love are more so poems about shit that felt like love, even though it wasn't. Most of my poems on love have been directly influenced by a person that has come into my life. Writing a poem about them allows me to capture how they made me feel, so I can either appreciate the aftertaste of our history or remind myself not to ever be within 100ft of them again. Sometimes I reread my work and gag because I wonder how I allowed myself to entertain certain situations. Undeniably, love (or the lack thereof) has taught me a lot about myself. Here's a look into my lessons:

Summer Skin

It was hot but
Your shade gave me safety
From the sun

Your pretty dark skin
Stuck to the car seat
In the summer heat

Your lips gave me
Traces of Popsicle passion
Our bodies would firecrack
In the back of my truck

Each time I reached out
To touch you
Your reaction gave me
Another reason to love you

We'd argue about
Who would get whose plate
At your uncles barbeque
But I'd always give in
Because I loved your pretty dark skin

With your hand on my thigh
I knew I could face anything
Even the Sharia law

I'd have gotten thrown
Off a building for you or stoned
As long as I didn't have to do it alone.

Aliens

Your words are like aliens
They've been flying
Over the heads of the ones that can't handle you
Like a candle, you burnt yourself out
Trying to shine past your self-doubt

But your aliens abducted me
And they invaded my ears
I found myself hovering over
The world I used to know

The corners of your mouth
Form the edges of the galaxy
Everyone else hears your words and thinks
Your existence is a fallacy.

But your aliens are loud
And they live inside me now
I hear them at my peaks and my valleys,
And even in the dark alleys
The edges of space couldn't contain you
And there's no place inside it that would claim you
You remain untamed.

Drunken Butterflies

When you spoke to me
You had butterflies on your breath
Soaked in Ciroc and singed with cigarellos
Butterflies imposing on my garden
You told me that I needed more flowers
As you picked the ones I had for someone else

I had never known meadows
Only front lawns arrested with concrete
Only grass stains on denim, and denim stains on dollar
bills
Only contribution to carelessness

Being careful with you
Meant never listening to a word you say
But I like butterflies
Isn't it love if they land on me?
Isn't a butterfly still beautiful if it has landed elsewhere
before me?
Or lands elsewhere after me?

I'd watch them spill from your lips
And cling to my skin
Of course, I wanted them to stay
I had never known meadows
Only front lawns and butterflies

Bad Trip

I can remember how we'd smoke squares after the white
Somehow, all those lines made you pointless
Somehow, I could only see clearly when I looked right
through you

You used to celebrate my smile like a holiday
Now I can only hear the interludes of your albums
The best somethings that didn't last long enough

I saw you in the gallery after I had waited in line so long
Once I got inside, I didn't want to see true color
I needed all the grayscale that would leave me guessing

Once I had you figured out, you were just another bad
trip
Every druggie has had you before

Love's ABC's

A - asking if I've eaten
B - binge watching a series together
C- calling my mother on her birthday
D- distracting my depression
E- entertaining my 17 personalities
F- FORGIVENESS
G- going the extra mile (duh)
H- holding a seat for me when I'm late
I - inside jokes
J- Jesus, at the center
K- knowing my favorite snack
L- late night car rides
M- making a pizza at 1am with me
N- never giving up on us
O- opening your mind
P- protecting me
Q- questioning my 2013 fashion
R- rubbing my back
S- stealing my lingo
T- telling me I can
U- understanding when I can't
V- verifying that I made it home safe
W- withstanding change
X- *don't compare me to him*
Y- yelling my name when I win
Z- zipping up baggage

Honey

This high we have is an odyssey
wrapped in honey

Your voice sounds like sunflowers
reaching up from the earth

And I find you watering them
with your words
I hate to disturb your verbs so
I just watch you sometimes

This is miles and miles of infatuation
in a drop top Pontiac
This is a journey through small towns
where who we are isn't welcomed
And yet, here we are together

Our love becomes aged wine, something
That only gets better with time.

Mothered by madness and fathered by
Forgiveness

Born from the quiet intersection of the two
I don't care where this road trip takes us
As long as I'm riding with you

2am

Don't know what I wanted from you

Love would be too easy to cry about

Maybe I wanted my value to be seen and sold

to the most deserving

Every time you stripped away my gold, I folded into
myself to find more

I reached into the deepest crevices of my potential and
gave you the best parts of me

You had the pleasure of finding the hidden treasures in
my soul

I gave you the map and you still lost me

Your love for me only showed itself in 2am texts

My love for you was always ready at 2am

I'd let your fingers run wild through my curls

I'd boast scents of masculinity and the salts of my skin
would float you like the Dead Sea

I protected our post-passion pillow talk in a fashion no
other man could mimic

I followed the directions of your confusion

I spoke fortitude into your damaged heart as I closed off the tomb to mine

In all of my distance and isolation, I was still available for you

The 2am tyrant

The ruler with immeasurable evasion, yet inches away from his own demise

Sometimes a dozen "2ams" would pass before I was summoned by you again

I brought everything I had to you at 2am

I left with nothing

I told myself that I was the one that wanted to go when it was obvious I couldn't stay the night

I would get home and realize that I had donated all of my wealth to a rich man

A man who was rich in all the wealth he had collected from others

Before me, during me, after me

Part of me wants to burst into your home and steal back all the bitter somethings I gave you

Part of me wants to write down all your sweet nothings and burn them in your face

I was poor for a long time after you

Begging myself for the change I wanted to get from you

Begging myself for the dollars I spent trying to look good for you

Begging myself for a start over

But now I ignore the 2am texts I would have been so happy about before

Instead I've somehow whispered wealth into my own heart, and I am richer than ever

I've claimed back all the wealth I'd left with you, because you no longer have access to it

You were the glitter that wasn't gold, nor silver, nor bronze

I found my gold and I gave it back to me

So now at 2am instead of waiting for you to give me purpose, I read your text and don't reply, on purpose.

Patience

I watched it eat you up
You used to fight back tears
And I kept telling you to stop the violence
I learned so much about you
During those late night car rides in silence
I asked God for guidance
As I got lost in you
Your Bermuda Triangle eyes

Every time I laid on your chest
I heard the ocean
Your breaths gently crashed into the top of my head
I knew all the ones that couldn't have you
Wanted you dead

I knew we'd built our palace on passion
But somehow it still feels real
I'd let you feed me lies just in case
It was my last meal

I would freeze them and try to save
Them for arguments we'd have later

Somehow, I know you'd always come back
Like a stray cat, or a package with the wrong address
I didn't want to address the girl who was wearing a dress
In your phone

But I had to

The one who has brunch with your mom
The mom I've never been introduced to
I only survived this ride with you
Because I don't mind traffic

Patience flows through me for you
And all of the bullshit you put me through
I know you love me
More than you love what the world tells you to love

I am more to you than a lie for your mother
I am your private destination
So please don't let the second guessing get to me
Before you do.

Stuck

We felt sunrises on the horizon of our lips
Exchanging a rose with each of the apologies
We juxtapose with unapologetic love
Fierce fear of feeling anything outside of each other
I take one look at you and see California beaches
Everyday you give me a new Frank Ocean line to relate
to
It's usually easy for me to run away
But to even walk away from you? I would hate to.

My Oak

We are trees swaying in the forest
If we fell for each other
Only God would hear it
The rest would be rumor
And ridicule
The rest would come
If we decide to never fall again
The birds would find another tree
Our leaves would shrivel into
Tiny pieces of folklore
Our branches might grow brittle
And our roots might dry
But damn it
We would still be trees

Sun Dress

The sky has let her hair down
Locks of lavender and curly blonde
She becomes a silent storyteller
Her smile gone until the morning beyond

Slowly she slips into her dark blue dress
And her sequins begin to shine
Swinging her cocaine white fur stole
As she dances with sunset's paradigm

I could watch her for hours
But if she cries, I'll get the best sleep
Never before have I seen a woman
Who can make music as she weeps

She wears what she wants
Comes and goes as she pleases
Whenever I make time to watch her
She smiles and time freezes

Condiment

God forbid I stumble upon
A condom meant for somebody else
I didn't ask to be the ketchup packet
In your letterman jacket
Forgotten for so long that I'd rather be used

Every fight we had was a weed growing strong
In the countryside sun
The warmth made it worse
I told myself goodbye a hundred times
So you wouldn't have to
So you'd stay

My favorite breath of fresh air
Dressed in carcinogens
Toxicity became intoxicating
Just like everything else about you

Maybe you found out that I really wasn't
From Mars
Instead I was a fossil
Just a print of something that was
Meant for a different time

You arrived late to the love I had for you
I spent Sundays in pews
Asking God for the right cues
To know when to leave you

You're a man of promise that wasn't kept
Just a man that kept promising
Just a man who prided himself
In all the ketchup packets he had collected

God forbid I become another condiment
For somebody else

God forbid I spend hours in the shower
Trying to wash you off

I told myself I wouldn't be that guy
I told "that guy" I wouldn't be that guy
Staring into your bathroom mirror
After I saw the condom meant for someone else

7. Wild Charcoal

Keep Swimming, Black Boy

I should probably start by saying that I am proud to be black and would never abandon my race. I find myself collateralizing my debts to my ancestors as I continue to assert and affirm my position in society. This "position" is indefinite, and continues to evade my grasp; it's the butterfly that I've been yearning to catch since childhood. I'd love to think that the ones who came before me are proud of my intent, if nothing else. I've heard a few people proclaim that African Americans don't have a tangible culture. Much of the African culture was lost during slavery, and the rest of it was diluted with European Catholicism. But somehow, we have managed to establish a monochromatic interpretation of what it means to be black; an interpretation that is garnished with stereotypical conjecture. Blackness in America is perceived like one medium sized, red jacket. Of course, this jacket won't fit everyone, and the red color will not satisfy everyone's preferences. As dogmatic and narrow as this interpretation might be, it has become the face of blackness both within the Black community and without. Sometimes I wonder if anyone in our community embodies this perception of Blackness, because I often find myself bending and breaking to fit into this jacket. I often try to force myself to like the color red. I imagine that on a lot of blacks, it must feel like wearing a straitjacket.

I ponder my own experience within my community. Sometimes I consider myself to be a "hybrid black". Not because I have mixed blood running though my veins (I am mostly of African descent), but because I have a diverse range of experiences. I grew up in two very different neighborhoods, and had exposure to contrasting perspectives of Black life. I grew up in a neighborhood called Beverly; with affluent Blacks who had exceptional socioeconomic stature. The other half of my childhood was spent in a neighborhood called Roseland; doused in poverty, lack of resources, and violence. Of course, this variation occurs across all races, but experiencing two different realms of Black culture made it difficult for me to determine my fit in the Black world. I had been told that being able to articulate your words and speak "proper" English would allow me to advance into spaces that are typically reserved for white people. I was also told that I was "talking white" when I applied proper English in my conversations with some of the people in my community. For a while, it seemed like true success meant disassociating with the red medium sized jacket Blackness. In the same regard, I also felt like true Blackness could only be achieved if one could fit into the red medium sized jacket; the mainstream Blackness.

There is blatant pressure within my community to succumb to the depictions of Black life that we see in the media. Perhaps these ideals serve as catalysts for cannibalism among us. It is unfortunate to see Blacks who are alienated or ostracized because of their Blackness that takes on a different form. Gender, sexuality, economic status, political view, and religious affiliation are just a few of the barriers that perpetuate division within our community. Being a minority within a minority has made me feel isolated and confused; struggling to wear my identity simultaneously with my Blackness has been a difficult experience. At times, the pressures of mainstream Blackness can be overwhelming.

I have been pressured to eat certain foods (and avoid others)

"You know Black people don't eat ____!"

I have been pressured to know how to dance.

I have been pressured to dress a certain way

I have been pressured to be cis gendered and straight

I have been pressured to be angry

- I've also been pressured to insert race into every aspect of my day, as if the world owes me something.

I have been pressured to be violent

I have been pressured to play basketball

- It doesn't help that I'm 6ft 3

I have been pressured to embrace certain genres of music (and avoid others)

i.e. "Blacks don't listen to that…" "What? You don't like R. Kelly??"

I have been pressured to avoid certain excursions, because these types of excursions are "for white people"

I have been pressured to disrespect women

I have been pressured to disrespect the police (without any substantial reason to do so)

-Although, due to ongoing incidents with police all over the country, this pressure (fear) can be partially justified

I have been pressured to "stop talking white" (didn't know white was a language)

As I struggled with my identity, I began to question if I would ever feel at home in my own community. Of course, there were many aspects of Black culture that I embodied, but there were also a few aspects of myself that did not oblige the uniformity of stereotypical Blackness. I wanted, so badly, to feel "at home" in my own skin, and in my own community. As I began to encounter other Blacks who were also feeling isolated, I realized that I was not the problem.

Our community needs to realize that, much like the actual color, there are different shades of Blackness. Our progression as a people in white capitalist America can only be attained through unity. It is important that we begin to nurture the Blacks who do don't fit into the red medium sized jacket of Blackness. The ones who are bending and breaking in their own skin for acceptance and sense of belonging. The Muslim Black. The LGBT Black. The disabled Black. The biracial Black. The Black who is a felon. The Republican Black. Hell, even the Trump supporting Black (yes, they exist). Within the walls of our community, we need to start acknowledging and affirming alternate expressions of "Blackness", combating the normalized projections of Blackness that we witness every day. A person should have the freedom to discover their identity outside of their skin color, and when they do; their skin color should still feel like the right fit. No more red medium sized jackets. No more bending and breaking.

Wild Charcoal

I battle depictions that
Are merely superstitions
My malleability resides
Only where I allow it

They want me to wear my black
Like a bruise
Hoping that one day
It'll fade away

But instead I wear my black
Like a fur coat
Burning through time
Shamelessly warm in the Arctic

Under my black lives
Relentless militant interior
I am protesting persecution
With my pride

I burn like wild charcoal
And they arrest my identity
But I found heaven in my handcuffs
I can burn with my hands behind my back

They think that I'm a masochist
Because I take my beatings and smile
They call me dirt
And forget about the garden growing from me

I am burning bridges
With the safeties of yesterday
Burning beyond my boundaries
My tears burning in my eyes

I'll burn as if nothing can tame me
Like wild charcoal

Sleepwalking *(Perspective is everything)*

(Read this poem from top to bottom, and then from bottom to top)

Black man wakes up
He wrestles with obligations until they win
He begins to get dressed and eat a balanced meal early
Prays for the day
He has ahead of him
All the demons and obstacles
Can no longer tune out
What must be heard
Man finds truth in
The Promise of God
Man refuses to believe
In fear, unless His face is shown
Man is acting
Out of frustration
Never settles for easy
Because it's wack to be the man who
Sells drugs and cracks cards
Works hard
Says he'll work hard to ensure he never
Becomes the statistic
Man is reduced to a statistic
Chooses to ignore it
Black man realizes there is still work to do

Black Boy Recipe

Prep time: (often skipped)

Cook time: The black boy spends time being "cooked" his whole life

Servings: Can feed the masses, if given a chance

For this recipe, you'll need the following ingredients:

3 chips on a shoulder (two are his own, and one from the shoulder he doesn't have to lean on)

Add 1 cup that holds all the tears the black boy is told he can't cry (and when he asks why, you begin to beat the mixture until he believes this lie)

You'll need 4-5 petals from the resilient flower that managed to grow through the concrete jungle

Next you'll add wise words from jailbirds and a good Sunday school lesson or two.

Add the rest of Trayvon Martin's Arizona, a few loose cigs from Eric Garner, and a toy gun from Tamir Rice

Keep this mixture away from the Heat, as it might just end the black boy's life

Don't let the mixture get diluted with evidence from the government that has been refuted

Add melanin, there is never too little or too much. There cannot be strength in a color if both ends of the spectrum are out of touch.

When the mixture becomes a man, he'll have to fight his way up from the bottom of the pan

No two batches are the same. We are not solely destined for prison, sports, or rap music. We are doctors, we are engineers, entrepreneurs. We are bilingual and we can be bisexual. We can feed the masses, if served with adequate representation and garnished with equal opportunity.

8. Red's Random Rants

Disclaimer: These are my opinions, but much of my arguments are substantiated by historical facts.

Racism:

Where should I start? Should I start by reminding America that technically everyone here, excluding the NATIVES, are immigrants? Although history books articulate the bone-chilling story of white imperialism time and time again, somehow there are some white Americans that feel like they own this land and hold rights to who inhabits it. Notice that I said "some". I'm not one of those *hotep*[4] extremists that relish in the belief that every white person, whether advertently or inadvertently so, is racist. I am beyond grateful for

---

[4] An African American male/female that has gotten carried away with their Afrocentrism. They substantiate their arguments with conspiracy theories and poorly researched facts. In their efforts to promote black progression, they often adopt misogynistic and homophobic notions.

the non-Black POC and the white Americans that stand at the forefront of the BLM movement, and use their platforms to rescind racism. Recognition and support from beyond our race is important for our progression as well.

Simple question. How can you really hate someone solely because of the color of their skin? How can you assume their value, their socioeconomic status, or even their right to live based on pigmentation? Before we address the imbecility of it all, let me formally declare that there are many shades of racism. Racism is like a box of chocolates, except that as a POC, you know that you will ALWAYS get a box of chocolates.
Let's take a peek at the variety:
You'll have the gun toting, Confederate flag flying racists that is somehow intelligent enough to own a construction company, and has sent numerous propositions to the Trump Administration with Mexico Border wall blueprints.
You have the racist that gets inexplicable anxiety whenever they have to share the sidewalk with a POC.

You have the racists that will hide behind Conservatism and patriotism to justify all of their anti-POC bullshit.

You have the racists that thinks "All Lives Matter" is a relevant movement.

Just in case I get bored with that variety, I can still look forward to being followed in the store, stopped and harassed by the police, being passive-aggressively shunned at work, or maybe not even being hired in the first place because of my race. So, I'll ask again…How could you possibly hate someone for an aspect of themselves that they can't control? To all the white people and non-Black POC who refuse to acknowledge the potency of racism, ask yourself this question: would you want to be an African American male in America right now? Would you want to be a Middle Eastern Muslim woman? (we'll cover this in my next rant). I'll wait. America is (on paper) a unique melting pot, with so much beauty in its diversity. However, years after slavery, segregation, immigration bans, etc., how much progress can we say we've really made? The question isn't rhetorical. America needs to stop trivializing the systematic oppression that is very real and very powerful.

Beyond racism, colorism is an adjacent issue that heightens the tension within minority communities. The normalization of fair skin has created a benchmark that has been overtly used for decades. If a person of color can "pass for white", they are greeted with more opportunity and inclusion. They are marketable and palatable to the world, and their darker skinned counterparts are left in the dust. Colorism breeds jealousy and division within the walls of a minority community. A Latina woman with Caucasian features (to no fault of her own), can abandon her Spanish and infiltrate the spaces of white America. Meanwhile, her cousin that is unmistakably Latina has to battle with prejudice constantly. There is a lingering preference for lighter skinned people of color within the walls of a race and beyond. Their beauty, intelligence, and class have become attached to the shade of their skin. This byproduct of racism proves that America values and prioritizes the fair skinned. However, within the walls of their communities, fairer skinned minorities have to battle with the assumptions made about them. "Oh, he thinks he's all that because he's light skinned." "She doesn't think she's black, or maybe she doesn't want to be!" In my opinion, I think colorism serves as a distraction as racism continues to thrive in America. Colorism is the conundrum that commands our attention for resolution. Part of the resolution should be less attention to skin color.

Sometimes I wonder if I'll ever be a priority in this country. As a black man, I have witnessed implicit racism. I have witnessed explicit racism. Racism is undeniable. We are told that if we don't like it, we should go back to Africa. We are told that Jim Crow is a thing of the past. We are told that we have access and opportunity just like everyone else in this country does.

Racism won't be resolved until everyone can feel at home in this country. It's 2018, and the progress that we've made as a nation is questionable. Of course I want to maintain my optimism, but this racist world can snatch that from you so quickly. It's exhausting to be hated and forgotten at the same time. Feeling like the last choice is exhausting, as well.

<u>Islamophobia:</u>

Let's face it; 9/11 added gallons of fuel to the
Islamophobic fire. It was the trauma that bigoted beasts
needed to justify their fear (hatred) of Middle Eastern
and Muslim Americans. Just as the TSA made extensive
adjustments to their security processes, our country made
adjustments to our capacity for prejudice. The media
crafted an image of treachery around the Islamic faith
and fed it's viewers a multitude of assumptive claims
about terrorism. I can only imagine the agony of hearing
my child ask me "Daddy, why are people staring at us?",
as I strap them into an aircraft. I can only imagine the
eyes around me piercing into my Middle Eastern skin
and assumptively crucifying me for my allegiance to ISIS.
It's dehumanizing.

Now in America, the Muslim religion and
Middle Eastern cultures are synonymous with terrorism.
I wish I was exaggerating, but I've overheard the anxious
dialogue in public places. I can only partially identify
with the harassment that Middle Eastern and Muslim
Americans face. I'm used to being stripped of my
harmlessness and clothed in crosshairs. I'm used to
being the elephant in the room, and being constantly

reminded that I don't belong. I'm used to my pigmentation being feared. But, lucky for me, I share my religion with the majority of Americans. Aside from occasional debates with atheist associates, I am rarely persecuted for being a Christian. To have your faith reduced to a terrorist movement is insulting and ridiculous. If one considered the frequency and potency of domestic terrorism in our nation today, there would be less concern about ISIS.

We have people in our own country who dislike other people in our country for attributes in which they either can't control, or shouldn't have to control. Harmful hatred of harmless people. Imagine being a victim of that almost every day of your life, because of what you wear, how you look, or who you praise. It has been over 16 years since September 11th, 2001, and yet some people still board a plane and get anxiety when they see a Middle Eastern man wearing a thawb or a dishdasha.

Homophobia/Transphobia:

Before I drag homophobes and transphobes to the moon and back, I must acknowledge that in my

120

adolescence and teenager years, I was a homophobe. I was raised to see the LGBTQ through a judgmental, unrealistic lens. It wasn't until I was faced with uncertainty about my own sexuality that I re-evaluated my perception on being gay. I can only begin to identify the tragedies of being a black queer person. The level of hatred and intolerance for it in our church ripples out into our community, and black queers find themselves being forced to disassociate from their own people. There is no room for us in black cishet culture, and no room for us in gay white culture. In our attempts to establish our own social and political organizations, we have been dismissed furthermore by the black cishet and white gay communities. They leave us to figure things out on our own.

Heteros underestimate the impact of homophobia and transphobia. A father in Henderson, Nevada killed his own 14 year old son because he was gay. Let's not forget the 49 people that were killed in a terrorist attack within the gay club "Pulse" in Orlando, Florida. 80% of violence against transwomen is violence against minority trans women. Gays and trans people are harassed and killed often, and it seems like there is little being done about it.

Listen, I know that for a straight person who has been marinating in heteronormative and gender-binary sauce all their life, it can be hard for them to comprehend what would make a person want to seek love from the same gender. On top of the fear that arises from not understanding it, you have religion fueling that fear and forming it into something hateful. Consensual homosexuality is illegal in 74 countries, and punishable by death in 12. This might be my American entitlement speaking, but how can we justify killing a man or woman that has consensual, age appropriate, non-predatory sex with a person of the same gender? Religion has a funny way of being a vehicle for either oppressive hatred or restorative intervention. As a God fearing Christian, I have come to the realization that at one point, the Bible was used to justify slavery. It was used (and is still used) to justify misogyny. I've had to adjust how I approach the Bible, because it can easily fuel a judgmental and intolerant mindset.

Another common argument used to refute queerness in the black community is the notion that black queer men are embracing emasculation. There is no doubt that there are ongoing efforts to rob the black man of his manhood. However, a man choosing to embrace his sexuality and gender fluidity is him taking the reins of his own life. There have been conversations about the image of the black man being exploited and altered in Hollywood. Conversations about the black man being portrayed in a feminine tint. Toxic masculinity tells us that anything outside the narrow margins of traditional masculinity is emasculation.

To consider that less than 100 years ago, Black People were considered $3/5^{th}$ human. Today, our lives are still valued as such. It baffles me that the same hyper masculine male that will call a gay male a slur (and possibly even attack him) will then later sheepishly reach out to him on a dating app in search of relations. This happens all the time, by the way. It also baffles me that the same minister that promotes hatred and intolerance of the LGBTQ will later be found guilty of molestation of children, or cheating on his wife with a girl that's probably half his age. It baffles me that when a black man doesn't identify with his current gender and transitions to womanhood, Black men suddenly feel like they have been personally attacked.

Of course, there has been progress in America; a lot of heteros like to bask in the fact that "the gays can get married now". How can the right to marry pacify us when there is undeniable, residual hatred that lingers in our country, not even mentioning the rest of the world? Social media has heightened my visibility to it (which is emotionally exhausting), new reports depict this hatred actualizing into violence, and I am still battling isolation from my family and in the workplace. Needless to say, these conditions make it difficult for one to be comfortable in their own skin. And yet people assume that we chose this lifestyle. Seems counterintuitive to choose a lifestyle that breeds oppression doesn't it?

<u>Misogyny:</u>

(as a male, I acknowledge my limited perspective.)

Internationally and almost universally, the functions and values of the "female" in our society are only appreciated when they are enabling patriarchy. For years, women have been flailing their arms in the periphery of men, in the periphery of the systems men have established, awaiting their equality. With their arms in the air, these women still manage to submit themselves to the expectations of their gender. They are bearing children. They are cleaning, cooking, and maintaining. They are cradling the heads of the very men that oppress them. Whispering affirmations into their ears. They are silencing the desires of their own heart. Whenever they use their arms for their own heart, they become controversial. Whenever they are leading, organizing, or taking action, men will concur that they have stepped outside of their rightful boundary. We have countless women in our society who have pioneered advances in different realms. Speakers. Innovators. Engineers. Healers. However, so many women are raised to believe that their purpose in life is to aid the advancement of men. In my environment, this concept is translated redundantly. Young boys often receive more attention in classrooms, and more encouragement in their homes. When women are sexually assaulted, the woman is often either doubted completely or blamed for what she did prior the assault. Our media projects body image turmoil into the minds of young girls, and they are objectified regardless of their reception/rejection of the pressure.

Growing up, I would often see my mother abide by my father's leadership. Her perception of her role as a wife was crafted by what the Bible told her a wife should be. My father would always have the final say, regardless if he was right or wrong. He was right because he was a man.

I have learned that many women are opposed to classical feminism, because it can be just as exclusive as the very systems it wants to dismantle. Women of color, women of lower social classes, and women of non-hetero sexuality are often overlooked (some would say ignored). Traditional feminism alleges inclusivity of all women, but seldom elevates the concerns of women who are oppressed for reasons beyond their gender. Is feminism solely for the uplifting of the white woman?

Harassment, sexual assault, gaps in compensation, and poor representation in the media are just a few of the major issues that women face today. In 2018. What will it take for minority women to gain access to the platforms of white feminism; when will we see more men participate in the uplifting and equalization of women? More unity will produce more solutions for women to thrive in patriarchal America.

I think that it is important to educate yourself about the oppression of the other minorities around you. In America, there are social issues that are swept under the rug every day. People are fearful about addressing them, especially if these issues do not affect them directly. Other people firmly deny the existence of these issues. However, I believe that the key to a more inclusive culture is intersectional solidarity. It is exhausting to be a minority. It seems as though you have to spend your whole life explaining/justifying/validating your existence to the majority. Many of us, are double and triple minorities; we remain aware of our repression as if it is the very air we breathe. We must move together. Iron sharpening iron.

I am challenging myself to understand the dilemmas of the people I share my country with. Embracing a more collectivist mindset. I challenge my readers to do the same.

Closing

Dear Reader,

I wanted to end on a positive note.

I am ecstatic that you took the time to learn my story. I hope that you feel less lonely and more whole. I am beyond confident that other people grapple with oppression daily (whether it manifests in the form of microaggression or blatancy). Despite the labels that the world might declare on you, I want you to know that you are worthy of happiness. You are worthy of love from yourself, your community, and the country that you reside in.

In the midst of me tackling everyday life, I've had time to ponder what I would like to change in my community, and in my country. I would like to see more synergy among minority groups. Theories of intersectionality teach us that oppression is multifaceted; it wraps around us in layers. However, if you are a minority within a minority, you should understand the importance of collaboration among the different groups.

The change starts with us. I am challenging myself to become more active in educating myself about other facets of oppression, ones that I haven't personally experienced. I am challenging myself to reach back into my community. I want to demand space for myself as I help others within it. Lastly, I am challenging myself to be Woodrow (the definition of that only truly matters to me and God). Anyone that knows me personally knows that I depreciate the importance of labels. I view labels as firm bricks for the barriers we build between one another.

Now go, be great and love freely.

Best,

Woodrow / Red / tbd

Afterword:

Wow.

I completed my first book.

I am so grateful for the people that told me that my poetry was powerful. Completing this collection was a major accomplishment, but going through with the publishing process was even more of a triumph for me. Putting my angst, my anger, my passion, and my soul into book form was a daunting process. Being vulnerable and open about my life is something that will hopefully touch and impact so many.

I realize that this book might reveal things about me to people that they never knew. Some people might be upset about some of my opinions and others might be shocked. But, I said what I said.

The question still stands: are you building bridges, or are you building barriers?

Thank you Mom and Dad, Zach, Asia, Ashley, Destinee, Diamond, Dr. Ayers, Tariq, Jessie. Thank you Zennie, I wish you could have the first copy. Thank you God.

Bibliography:

Welford , Judith, and Jane Powell. "A Crisis in Modern Masculinity: Understanding the Causes of Male Suicide." *Campaign Against Living Miserably*, 17 Apr. 2015, www.thecalmzone.net/2014/11/masculinity-audit/.

Made in the USA
Columbia, SC
16 January 2021